W9-CHK-566

The Shaping of a Man of Faith

The Shaping of a Man of Faith

Ben E. Ferguson

While this book is designed for the reader's personal enjoyment and profit, it is also intended for group study. A Leader's Guide is available from your local bookstore or from the publisher at $.75.

221.92
~~234.2~~

534

VICTOR BOOKS
a division of SP Publications, Inc., Wheaton, Illinois
Offices also in Fullerton, California; Whitby, Ontario, Canada • London, England

PROPERTY OF
BETHANY CHURCH LIBRARY
ROUTE 203
WYCKOFF, NEW JERSEY

Unless otherwise noted, Scripture quotations are from *The New American Standard Bible* (NASB), © 1960, 1962, 1963, 1968, 1971, 1972, 1973 by the Lockman Foundation, La Habra, California. Other quotations are from *The Living Bible* (LB), © 1971 by Tyndale House Publishers, Wheaton, Illinois. All quotations used by permission.

Recommended Dewey Decimal Classification: 221.924 or 234.2

Suggested subject headings: Abraham; Christian biography; Faith

Library of Congress Catalog Card Number: 78-55178
ISBN: 0-88207-516-0

© 1979 by SP Publications, Inc. All rights reserved
Printed in the United States of America

VICTOR BOOKS
A division of SP Publications, Inc.
P.O. Box 1825 • Wheaton, Ill. 60187

Contents

Foreword

The life of Abraham has been of perennial interest to Jews, Christians and Moslems. His life is set forth with such fulness in the Scriptures that the purpose of God must be that we should be edified by it.

Pastor Ben Ferguson has done a beautiful piece of work in tying together the different facets of the life of this great man of God into a beautiful whole in such a way that all is made to bear directly upon our life in Christ now. Those who call for more relevance in Bible teaching will surely find it here.

Pastor Ferguson has written with a warm heart toward his congregation and all who hear the message of God. The Lord's blessing is upon his oral ministry, as we pray it may be upon this written ministry.

CHARLES LEE FEINBERG
Dean, Talbot Theological Seminary

¹ Now the Lord said to Abram, "Go forth from your country, and from your relatives and from your father's house, to the land which I will show you.² And I will make you a great nation, and I will bless you, and make your name great." . . . ⁵ And Abram took Sarai his wife and Lot his nephew, and all their possessions which they had accumulated, and the persons which they had accumulated in Haran; and they set out for the land of Canaan. . . . ⁶ And Abram passed through the land as far as the site of Shechem, to the oak of Moreh. Now the Canaanite was then in the land.⁷ And the Lord appeared to Abram and said, "To your descendants I will give this land." So he built an altar there to the Lord who had appeared to him. . . .⁹ And Abram journeyed on, continuing toward the Negev.   Genesis 12:1-9

1

A Good Beginning

A baby's cry in the delivery room begins the long process of growing to maturity. Parents, anxious to care for their newborn, plan for the proper diet, dress, and home life. They want their new child to have a good beginning because patterns established in the crib influence behavior later in life.

Our commitment to helping a child get a good start in life reminds us of the spiritual parallel. Scripture uses the physical birth and life process as a striking illustration of the spiritual birth and life.

Just as a good beginning in our physical life is important, so the same is needed for a healthy spiritual life. Experience shows that trends established in the spiritual crib influence spiritual adolescent and adult behavior.

The question is: What makes a good spiritual beginning? The answer springs from the experience of one of the greatest men of faith—Abraham. This is the man who, on Mount Moriah, was poised to plunge a knife into the chest of his beloved son, Isaac. But while most recall Mount Moriah, few realize the intensity of the years of struggles preparing him for that event.

Studying Abraham's early experience of faith, we find four principles that guided him to the spiritual maturity of his later life. These principles can start us on the road toward our own Mount Moriah.

Initial Trust

Our first cry of faith comes in the spiritual delivery room. Trust in Christ is the first step in a long walk toward maturity. Fortunately, Abraham's moment of initial trust is recorded in the twelfth chapter of Genesis.

I find the narrative encouraging, for Abraham came from a background similar to ours. Before God called him to faith, he lived in Ur of the Chaldees, a city marked by prosperity and paganism.

Ur was located on the Euphrates River. Years of flooding brought silt deposits and made it a fertile farming area. A harbor town, it was a city of commerce in touch with world markets.

It was also a city whose people worshiped several gods. Ur was built around a large mound of dirt called a ziggurat. On top of the mound was a temple built for moon worship.

Circumstances are not much different now than in Abraham's day. We may not worship the moon, but we don't always worship God either. Prosperity continues to lavish creature comforts on us, in greater abundance than in any time in history.

At the same time we are experiencing a revival of the ancient idolatries known to Abraham. Astrology, witchcraft, black magic, and a host of their evil cohorts continue to claim greater numbers of followers.

Although tradition of the ancient East suggests that Abraham refused to take part, his family enjoyed the wealth and idolatry of the city. It is possible that Abraham did not participate, but we have no proof that he was any different from others (Josh. 24:2).

Then one day the God of Glory appeared and invited Abraham to trust in Him. The call in no way reflected on the personal goodness of Abraham. God did not look down from heaven and say, "Abraham seems like a nice guy. He doesn't seem quite as bad as the rest. I'll ask him to follow Me." It was not like that then, or now. God never asks us to follow Him because of what we can do for Him, but because of what He can do for us.

The call to Abraham showed God's sovereign purpose. When Adam and Eve sinned, God planned to redeem fallen man through Christ. "And I will put enmity between you and the woman, and between your seed and her seed; He shall bruise you on the head, and you shall bruise him on the heel" (Gen. 3:15).

Abraham was a link in the chain of the family through which Christ would come. Abraham's role in God's program was revealed when God said: "For I have chosen him in order that he may command his children and his household after him to keep the way of the Lord by doing righteousness and justice; in order that the Lord may bring upon Abraham what He has spoken about him" (Gen. 18:19).

God invited Abraham, an unbeliever, to trust Him and become a part of His plan of redemption. God still invites men who worship wealth and modern idols to exercise faith in Christ. None of us are called to Christ because of our worthiness or potential for service. Isaiah wrote that in God's sight, all our goodness is like a pile of filthy rags (Isa. 64:6). We are chosen because God sovereignly decided to call us. Paul's words deflate the ego of self-important men: "just as He chose us in Him before the foundation of the world, that we should be holy and blameless before Him" (Eph. 1:4). Exercising His sovereign will, God chose us even before we were born and had any opportunity to demonstrate how worthy we would be to Him.

Just as Abraham was chosen to fulfill part of the sovereign plan of God, we too have been chosen for a divine purpose. Jesus declared, "You did not choose Me, but I chose you, and appointed you, that you should go and bear fruit, and that your fruit should remain" (John 15:16).

He appoints us to live for Him and to share the life-giving Gospel of salvation. Our initial trust is the foundation for a good beginning in our Christian life.

A New Life-style

A new life-style is another necessity for the pilgrimage toward spiritual maturity. The change in the life-style of Abraham was sketched in these words: "Now the Lord said to Abram, 'Go forth from your country, and from your relatives, and from your father's house, to the land which I will show you; and I will make you a great nation, and I will bless you, and make your name great; and so you shall be a blessing; and I will bless those who bless you, and the one who curses you I will curse. And in you all the families of the earth shall be blessed'" (Gen. 12:1-3).

He was told to leave his native land and become a man without a country. God wanted him to break tradition by leaving his father's house and become a man without a family. Abraham would also have to renounce the gods of Ur and worship a new God.

Abraham could have strongly objected to following God. What 75-year-old man in his right mind would pull up stakes to start a new life? Besides, Abraham had made a very good life for himself. Why should he follow the advice of someone he could not even see?

Was God being unfair? No! Separation from the old life has definite benefits. Once isolated from old friends and associates, Abraham would be forced to depend on God alone. Further, the blessings of God's promises depended on complete separation from the old life.

After our first act of trust, God expects us to adopt a new life-style. In God's sight, our old life is gone and is replaced with the new life found in Christ. "Therefore if any man is in Christ, he is a new creature; the old things passed away; behold, new things have come" (2 Cor. 5:17).

The new Christian life-style includes Christ in its planning and thinking as His Word is read. It may even call for a new occupation as it did for one man in his mid-forties. One year after coming to Christ, God called him to change occupations. Immediately, steps were taken to sell his business and enroll in seminary in preparation for his new occupation—proclaiming the Gospel of Christ.

When we grasp the radical change God desires in our lives, we might suspect God of being unfair in His demands. We might be tempted to say, "Change my plans? Sorry, God, I made these plans long before I knew You and I don't intend to change them for anybody."

Changes may seem extreme, but they are essential. Until the new life-style emerges we will never develop dependence upon God. Isolation from old friends and associations forces us to rely on Him more.

God's promises are a great incentive for us to change. God asked a lot from Abraham, but He promised a great deal in return. In place of the land he left, Abraham was promised a new land; in place of his relatives, he was promised that he would father a great nation.

In addition, God promised he would become a blessing to the whole earth: "in you all the families of the earth shall be blessed" (Gen. 12:3). How strange this must have sounded to Abraham, who at 75 was still tied to his father Terah's apron strings. He had not been free to be a blessing to anyone, but God promised that he would bless the entire world!

God does not ask us to give up more than He is willing to give us in return. Peter wrote: "Seeing that His divine power has granted to us everything pertaining to life and godliness, through the true knowledge of Him who called us by His own glory and excellence. For by these He has granted to us His precious and magnificent promises, in order that by them you might become partakers of the divine nature, having escaped the corruption that is in the world by lust (2 Peter 1:3-4).

It is exciting to think about what God promises us. He promises us a new family—the family of all believers (Rom. 8:17); a new home—our citizenship is in heaven (Phil. 3:20); and a new occupation—bearing fruit for God (John 15:16). Indeed, we are just passing through this world waiting till Jesus tells us our place in heaven is ready.

Obedience

Obedience is the next necessity for our spiritual pilgrimage. Abraham's obedient response to God's call is recorded in Genesis 12:4-5.

Without hesitation or debate, Abraham obeyed. "By faith Abraham, when he was called, obeyed by going out to a place which he was to receive for an inheritance; and he went out, not knowing where he was going" (Heb. 11:8).

The quick unhesitating move in heading for an unknown destination showed obedience to God's command. Actually his obedience was incomplete. God said, "Go forth from your country and from your *relatives*" (Gen. 12:1). We read, "So Abram went forth as the Lord had spoken to him; and Lot went with him" (Gen. 12:4). As he headed for the land, nephew Lot was tagging along.

As Abraham moved out to claim the promise of his new life, he brought along part of the old life in the person of Lot. He wanted to claim the blessings without obeying all the commands. The consequences of incomplete obedience were not immediate, but they were big.

If Lot had been left behind in Ur, Abraham's camp would not have experienced dissension (Gen. 13:7). Also, Abraham could have avoided going to war to rescue Lot from foreign invaders (Gen. 14). If Lot had not been along, his incestuous encounter with his daughters, which produced the Moabite and Ammonite peoples, probably never would have happened (Gen. 19:30-38).

In the long run, taking Lot along caused Abraham much anxiety and difficulty. He was in the land a long time, but he did not enjoy it until Lot was gone. Even then his peace was frequently interrupted, because Lot had a talent for getting into trouble. Experience taught Abraham that God demands complete obedience.

Trusting Christ means claiming God's offer for eternal life. However, to enjoy fully our new relationship with God, we must be completely obedient to Him. Jesus said, "You are My friends, if you do what I command you" (John 15:14).

Each command in the New Testament is placed there for our benefit. God, in His omniscience, knows we need to meet regularly with other believers for spiritual strength (Heb. 10:25); that we need to communicate with Him in prayer (Heb. 4:16); and that we need to study His Word (2 Tim. 2:15).

Deliberately ignoring or disobeying commands from God will bring unpleasant results. Refusal to study the Bible brings a loss of divine direction. Failure to fellowship with other believers is a prelude to personal problems. One of the sad parts of a counseling ministry is seeing the number of believers who get into sin as a result of dropping out of regular participation in a local assembly.

J. H. Sammis was right on target when he wrote, "Trust and obey, for there's no other way to be happy in Jesus, but to trust and obey." Abraham experienced this and so do we.

Open Confession

Open confession of faith is also needed if we are to reach spiritual maturity. Abraham's decision to follow God was put on public display before his relatives and friends. It is unlikely that he waited until dark to fold his tents and slip quietly out of Haran so that no one would find out. Everyone who knew Abraham knew that he was going to a "new land" following a "new God."

It is also unlikely that his family and friends

understood what he was doing. If Abraham had announced that he was moving away to accept a job offer that promised more pay, that would have been easier to accept. But to give up everything to become a homeless wanderer, never! His family did not understand his new life or his commitment to God.

His stand for God was made known to the inhabitants of the new land upon his arrival. "And Abram passed through the land as far as the site of Shechem, to the oak of Moreh. Now the Canaanite was then in the land. And the Lord appeared to Abram and said, 'To your descendants I will give this land.' So he built an altar there to the Lord who had appeared to him. Then he proceeded from there to the mountain on the east of Bethel, and pitched his tent, with Bethel on the west and Ai on the east; and there he built an altar to the Lord and called upon the name of the Lord" (Gen. 12:6-8).

The oak of Moreh was a place where the occult arts were practiced. As a newcomer in the land, living among a people who were involved in occult practices, Abraham did not keep quiet about his faith in God.

Abraham declared his allegiance immediately, by building an altar to the Lord. He moved further into the land, building another altar and calling on the name of the Lord. In so doing he openly confessed to the residents (Canaanites) in the area that he, a newcomer, was a follower of God.

When Jesus Christ called His followers, He did

it publicly, reminding them of the necessity of confessing Him before men. He did not want secret disciples. When John the Baptist asked for converts, he made a public display of their baptism.

God expects the same response today. I am not suggesting that you build an altar on Main Street and bow down there calling on the name of God. Nevertheless, our faith must be confessed openly before men.

When Paul wrote about confessing with the mouth, (Rom. 10:9-10), he was referring to an experience similar to Abraham's altar. Paul meant that we are to tell our friends and business associates that we know Christ and are following Him.

Openly confessing our faith strengthens us. It helps us verbalize what we believe, enabling us to tell others about Christ with greater ease. It is also an act of declaring our allegiance to Christ, thus giving added strength in times of difficulty.

If we hope to make much progress in our Christian lives, we need a good beginning. After that, with proper care, our faith begins to grow.

[10] Now there was a famine in the land; so Abram went down to Egypt to sojourn there. . . .[11] He said to Sarai his wife, "See now, I know that you are a beautiful woman. . . .[13] Please say that you are my sister so that it may go well with me because of you, and that I may live on account of you." . . . [15] And Pharaoh's officials saw her and praised her to Pharaoh; and the woman was taken into Pharaoh's house. [16] Therefore he treated Abram well for her sake. . . .[17] But the Lord struck Pharaoh and his house with great plagues because of Sarai, Abram's wife. [18] Then Pharaoh called Abram and said, "What is this you have done to me? Why did you not tell me that she was your wife? [19] Why did you say, 'She is my sister,' so that I took her for my wife? Now then here is your wife, take her and go." . . . [13:1] So Abram went up from Egypt to the Negev, he and his wife and all that belonged to him; and Lot with him. . . .[3] And he went on his journeys from the Negev as far as Bethel, to the place where his tent had been at the beginning, between Bethel and Ai,[4] to the place of the altar, which he had made there formerly; and there Abram called on the name of the Lord. Genesis 12:10—13:4

2

Faith in Crisis

An Air Traffic Controller shoulders heavy responsibilities when he sits at his radar console. He is responsible for the pilots' and passengers' lives, as well as for the multimillion-dollar airplanes flying through his control sector.

Although the pilot never sees the controller, he would not think of flying without him. His man on the ground relays vital information and directs his course along the way. With the controller guiding the aircraft and the pilot obeying the controller's orders, the two make an effective example of mutual trust.

The possibility always exists that a pilot will be tempted to trust his own common sense rather than follow instructions from the controller. That is a serious mistake and could get the pilot in deep trouble with the Federal Aviation Administration.

Still worse, independent action endangers the lives of the passengers aboard his aircraft.

The dependence of a pilot on his unseen controller provides an excellent example of a basic principle of faith: Follow God's direction rather than your own natural instincts.

God, though unseen, is our traffic controller. He provides vital information and warns us about course corrections, rough weather, and other approaching aircraft in our flight plan. We make a faith team, as God gives directions and we carry them out. The rules of faith dictate that we follow His orders instead of trusting our own judgment.

Of course, even though we are following God, we still have that other little voice inside us. It begins as a whisper and works its way up to full volume. It says, "How do I know that God won't make me do something that I hate? Besides, I know how I want to live my life and I don't need someone else to run it for me." The little voice is so easy to listen to and so easy to believe. But that mistake gets us into trouble with God. And worse yet, our independence can adversely affect the lives of others.

Abraham was one who, when faced with a difficult problem, chose to follow his own instincts rather than trust God.

Doing What Comes Naturally

A basic fact of the Christian life is that we will face difficult situations called "crisis experiences." The question is not "If" a crisis comes, but rather

"When?" We all get chances to cope with crisis experiences.

As Abraham traveled from his homeland in Ur, he was ignorant of the crisis he was to experience on his arrival. In simple trust, Abraham renounced all that was rightfully his in Ur, traveled cross-country on foot to Canaan and openly confessed his allegiance to God.

But reality has a way of hitting us squarely in the face when we least expect it. Abraham's moment of truth came when he surveyed his new home and faced the stark facts. The text says, "Now there was a famine in the land" (Gen. 12:10). The hills and valleys of the Promised Land were parched and barren.

Abraham, as tribal head, was responsible for the life and health of many servants, in addition to large herds and flocks. The famine ravaging the land produced a food shortage both for man and beast. His responsibility to provide for his family, servants, and herds in a land racked by shortage produced a crisis for his faith.

Abraham faced a practical problem of enormous proportions. His economic and physical survival were at stake in the strange land where God had led him. With each passing day his servants and herds consumed more of the available food supplies, thus intensifying matters.

Facing a crisis of survival, Abraham had to make a decision—and soon—if he and his herds were to survive. Three courses of action were considered. He could stay in the Promised Land where God had led him and trust Him to feed the livestock. However, that did not make sense. God had led him from the fertile regions of Ur and deposited him in the midst of a land wasting away by famine. Now it appeared that God had abandoned him. Sitting in Canaan facing the prospect of starvation for his herds, he might have uttered, "And for THIS I gave up the security of Ur." No, it did not make sense to sit and starve. The gravity of the crisis demanded sensible action.

Abraham could have returned to Ur where he had relatives and friends who could help him get reestablished. But his departure from Ur to follow God to a new land made that difficult. Returning to Ur would mean admitting that he had made a mistake and that his new God could not meet his needs. His pride would not permit returning to face the ridicule and snide remarks of his friends. Death in Canaan was preferred to the shame of Ur.

Or, Abraham could move on to another land looking for "greener pastures." This would surely beat starving in Canaan or the ridicule of returning to Ur, and it made good sense.

As the pressure mounted, it became too great for Abraham. He observed others moving south to escape the famine, so he followed suit. ". . . So Abram went down to Egypt to sojourn there, for the famine was severe in the land" (Gen. 12:10). Our hero who had 75 years experience in going his own way, walked by sight as he followed the crowd to Egypt.

In making his practical decision, he overlooked the promises God made in Ur. God directed him to Canaan, but he did not consult God before leaving for Egypt. Abraham relied on his own ingenuity and did the logical thing—he looked for new grazing lands.

It takes little imagination to see how he reached his decision. As a new believer, Abraham had not yet learned that God could be trusted to provide his daily bread. God promised nothing about his cattle. But the real clincher came with the thought of saving God's honor. If Abraham did not survive in Canaan, what good was the promise that he would be a blessing to the whole earth? Feeling let down and abandoned by God, the pressure of the food shortage prompted him to make every effort to guarantee his survival.

Challenges to Faith

If his experience were not so painfully familiar, we might be tempted to point an accusing finger at Abraham for abandoning God when the going got tough. But our lives are not without crisis experiences. Although we know that our eternal destiny is secure, we often get edgy and we doubt —especially when a family member faces unemployment, a close friend fights a terminal illness, or a loved one is suddenly an innocent victim of a tragic accident.

Unexplainable events that seem to have no purpose challenge our willingness to trust God. In reality the big crises we face are *practical*, not *theological.* Our security is threatened more by the stock market than by a new concept in theology.

When practical crises *do* come, we have the same options that Abraham faced. We can sit still and wait for God to act. Or we can listen to that little voice inside and agree that God really has no idea what is happening to us.

If we listen to that little voice, it won't be long before we are sure that God has failed. Sheepishly, we can admit to our unbelieving friends that God has gone back on His promise, and turn to them for help. But this is not the easy way out, especially if we want to maintain our mask of spirituality.

If we think that waiting for God to act is useless, we can always solve the problem by taking matters into our own hands. We can look around and see what others are doing and then do something similar to relieve our own situation. This seems to be the most popular solution when we face a crisis.

It is easy to forget God when the piercing pain of problems stabs at us. If, as we reason, God is not really interested in our hurts, then we might as well solve our own problems.

In our own ingenuity we change jobs to make more money; move to a new region in search for better employment; or fall into a "get rich quick" scheme that is guaranteed to work. Frequently we do what comes naturally. After all, we have more experience in that than in trusting God.

A businessman shared the following story. God had so blessed his business that during the first three months of the year he met the company's annual sales quota. He felt quite good about it and used a great deal of his time serving the Lord. One month he took a trip away doing the Lord's work. In returning to his business, he discovered the bottom had dropped out! His falling sales were less than half of the normal. In a moment of anxiety he set out to solve the problem himself and reverse the slumping sales curve. He confessed that he had not even thought to turn to God for direction, but had taken practical steps to solve his problem. Sounds familiar, doesn't it?

When we take drastic action on our own, it is an admission that we have forgotten God, and have become so involved in our problem that we don't even think about Him. It is easy to do the natural things, but a Christian is more than a natural man. Doing what comes naturally often is a practical denial of trust in the living God.

Counting the Cost

Everything has a price tag. I have frequently heard the old saying, "If you want to dance you'll have to pay the fiddler." It's true. Everything has a cost that must be counted.

Abraham learned this painful truth when he tried to solve his problem. His trip to Egypt represents turning to the world for help. Egypt apparently had escaped the ravages of famine and in her prosperity, she fostered an open door policy toward refugees from drought-stricken Canaan. Those seeking aid found it in Egypt. Abraham, ignoring the promises and the place of blessing, turned to the world for survival.

The first cost of his decision was deceit. Abraham adopted a new philosophy as he turned away from God—worry. As they approached Egypt, fear gripped his soul. Wise in the ways of the world, he knew that his life was at stake. He said to Sarah, "See now, I know that you are a beautiful woman; and it will come about when the Egyptians see you, that they will say, 'This is his wife'; and they will kill me, but they will let you live. Please say that you are my sister so that it may go well with me because of you, and that I may live on account of you" (Gen. 12:11-13).

Fearing for his own skin and living by his wits, he concocted a plan which involved his wife in lying for him. Actually, Sarah was not really lying, for she was a half sister to Abraham (Gen. 20:12).

First, he failed to trust God for food, then he could not trust Him for his life. If God could not provide food for the livestock, Abraham believed that God could not keep them safe in Egypt. Besides, what good were God's promises about a great nation if Abraham's body was rotting in the Egyptian soil?

Abraham was right. As soon as they arrived in Egypt, word of Sarah's beauty reached the king. Anxious to add her to his harem, he sent lavish gifts to Sarah's "brother" as a dowry.

It worked! Because Abraham "outwitted" the Egyptians, he survived and lived in Egypt where ample grain was available for his herds. He also had more wealth and new status as "brother-in-law" to the king.

It seems this action makes a liar of those who argue that sin doesn't pay. Abraham could testify that his deceit paid off handsomely. At least it looked that way on the surface.

However, the dividends of deceit must be weighed against the hidden costs. Abraham's experience in Egypt was expensive. Imagine how Abraham felt as he sat alone at night and thought of his beloved Sarah in the royal harem. In the loneliness of his quiet tent, his survival, wealth, and status were poor substitutes for Sarah.

Further, God's blessings promised to Abraham were for the land God showed him. Sitting in Egypt, he was out of the Promised Land so he had no blessing from God.

A final cost was the loss of fellowship with God. While in Egypt he built no altar, nor did he call on the name of the Lord. The trip may have been practical, but it cost Abraham his fellowship with God.

No wife, no blessing, and no fellowship were costs far outweighing the benefits received. As a young believer, Abraham needed to learn that God could provide for the practical needs of life.

It is easy to identify with this experience. In our crisis experiences we often turn to the world for help. We have more experience in the ways of the world than in the ways of God. Rather than giving God a chance, we follow the newest trend.

On the surface, living by our wits may pay handsome dividends. We may get the job that pays more money. With it we are able to buy a bigger house, save for the children's college years, enjoy more prestige in the community and even help support another missionary.

But is it really worth it? I would not advise running off on your own without counting the hidden costs. A move rips you up from your roots and transplants you in a new community, bringing loneliness caused by giving up close friends and church ties.

Acting without God's direction results in loss of fellowship with God. We can only enjoy His blessing and fellowship as long as we are in the place He assigns us. Any other place will bring misery.

A friend, on graduation from seminary, packed his furniture and moved his family to the area he had chosen. He admits now that he had no leading from God in the matter. When he arrived in the community, it was not long before he landed the position he wanted. Instead of the expected happiness, that job proved a source of heartache until he left within the year. He learned that moving without God's direction resulted in distress.

Picking Up the Pieces

Wise parents realize that mistakes are part of growing up. A child who is never permitted to make mistakes and learn from them will not be equipped to cope as an adult. God also permits His children to make mistakes as part of our spiritual education. As we pick up the pieces, God expects us to learn from our failures.

God made it possible for Abraham to pick up the pieces of their relationship when He intervened. Abraham was helpless to remedy the situation. "But the Lord struck Pharaoh and his house with great plagues because of Sarai, Abram's wife" (Gen. 12:17).

Even a godless king recognized divine intervention. He summoned Abraham, rebuked him for his deceit, and evicted him from the land. Abraham could have been killed, but instead he was deported as God overruled the understandable fury of the king.

With nowhere else to go, Abraham went back to Bethel, "to the place of the altar which he had made there formerly; and there Abram called on the name of the Lord" (Gen. 13:4). Scripture does not record the emotions of the first prodigal son's homecoming. It must have been a tender moment when Abraham returned to God who had been waiting for him all along.

At the altar in Bethel, Abraham picked up the pieces of a broken relationship by coming back to God, finding fellowship restored and the avenue of blessing open once again. Although forgiven and restored, the effects of his Egyptian folly plagued Abraham and his descendants from that day forward.

It encourages us to know that when we go away from God, He never goes away from us. He is still in the same place that He was before we turned away from Him. We can return to Him and find our fellowship restored.

Like Abraham, it may take divine intervention to bring us to our senses. Peter was rebuked by a crowing rooster and Balaam by a talking donkey, so it is not unreasonable that God might use the sharp words of an unbeliever to shock us back to the reality of our need for Him.

Once God wakes us up to the folly of going our own way, He restores our fellowship and blessing. His prescription for contemporary prodigals is "If we confess our sins, He is faithful and righteous to forgive us our sins and to cleanse us from all unrighteousness" (1 John 1:9).

Even though we find forgiveness and renewed fellowship, we may have to live with the results of our sin. A person who abuses his body, to the point where his health is broken, will have to suffer the consequences the rest of his life even though the sin is forgiven.

Joe had everything that would make a man happy: a family, a lovely home, and a good job with a national firm. But one day he announced that God had called him to the ministry and that he was leaving for seminary.

He quit his job, sold his home, bid farewell to his relatives and friends and moved his wife and children 2,000 miles to another city. After he arrived and enrolled in classes, he was unable to find work. His reserves were dwindling and something would have to be done soon to pay the bills and feed the family.

He could have returned to California and found his old job waiting. But that would have meant facing his family and admitting that God did not provide in the place where He had led. Joe could have dropped out of school and secured employment in his field of engineering. None of us would have faulted him for that action.

His only other option was to wait and claim God's promise to provide what his family needed. On the surface that seemed illogical, since God had let him down so far. After prayer, he announced his intention to stay in school. God *did* provide! Today he and his family serve God as missionaries in Latin America.

In the crucible of daily experience, Joe learned that God is concerned about the practical problems faced by a man and with a family, and that where God guides, He provides.

⁵ Now Lot, who went with Abram, also had flocks and herds and tents. ⁶ And the land could not sustain them while dwelling together. . . . ⁸ Then Abram said to Lot, "Please let there be no strife between you and me. . . . ⁹ Is not the whole land before you? Please separate from me: if to the left, then I will go to the right; or if to the right, then I will go to the left." ¹⁰ And Lot lifted up his eyes and saw all the valley of the Jordan, that it was well watered everywhere ʾ. . . like the garden of the Lord, like the land of Egypt as you go to Zoar. ¹¹ So Lot chose for himself all the valley of the Jordan. . . . ¹² Abram settled in the land of Canaan, while Lot settled in the cities of the valley, and moved his tents as far as Sodom. ¹³ Now the men of Sodom were wicked exceedingly and sinners against the Lord. ¹⁴ And the Lord said to Abram, after Lot had separated from him, "Now lift up your eyes and look from the place where you are, northward and southward and eastward and westward; ¹⁵ for all the land which you see, I will give it to you and to your descendants forever." . . . ¹⁸ Then Abram moved his tent and came and dwelt by the oaks of Mamre, which are in Hebron, and there he built an altar to the Lord.   Genesis 13:5-18

3

The Pull of the Pocketbook

Most people spend a lot of time worrying about their pocketbooks. The money drain causes us to think about how to make ends meet, how to make more to meet rising costs, and how to hang onto what we've gained.

Our pocketbooks are the objects of a giant tug of war. On one side, forces tug to pull our money away from us, while we tug furiously to keep a firm grip on the little wad of money we have. While fretting and fuming over money, we are unaware that our confidence in God's ability to take care of us is gradually disappearing.

Financial problems choke our trust in God. Jesus warned of this when He said the Word may be choked by the "worries of the world, and the deceitfulness of riches, and the desires for other things" (Mark 4:19). By experience we know the conflict between trusting God and taking care of our goods. We can learn from Abraham who, when experiencing money problems, trusted God.

Pocketbook Problems

We have all heard the saying, "Money isn't everything, but it's way ahead of whatever's in second place." That saying presents the notion that money solves our problems.

Abraham's difficulties relating to his wealth certainly dispelled that myth. He was a man with a big pocketbook, "very rich in livestock, in silver, and in gold" (Gen. 13:2). In addition he also had many servants who tended his herds. When he was in Egypt, his financial picture brightened because the king "gave him sheep and oxen and donkeys and male and female servants and female donkeys and camels" (Gen. 12:16).

But when he went back to Canaan, he faced a severe financial crunch. The land was still in ruin because of the famine. Abraham, who had a large livestock herd, lost money every day until sufficient grazing was available. The problem intensified because Lot "also had flocks and herds and tents" (Gen. 13:5).

This shortage triggered a major crisis. "The land could not sustain them while dwelling together, for their possessions were so great" (Gen. 13:6). This fostered hostility between the servants who disputed over grazing rights. It was just a matter of time before Abraham and Lot would clash.

This serious problem had spiritual overtones.

Here was another opportunity for Abraham to trust God. When facing a similar problem earlier, he fled to Egypt looking for help. Now back in the same situation, he had a second chance to prove he had learned his lesson.

But there was something more involved. Tucked neatly into the story are these words: "Now the Canaanite and the Perizzite were dwelling then in the land" (Gen. 13:7). Abraham had to consider what a dispute would mean to his unbelieving neighbors, since they knew that he worshiped a new God. If he and Lot fought it out, it would prove to their neighbors that this different God was not really as powerful as Abraham had said.

We face a problem very similar to Abraham's. Money famines come and demand an exercise of faith. Inflation eats away at the pocketbook. As prices increase and income remains steady, our money disappears like the grass on the parched hillsides of Canaan. Other problems like unemployment, installment payments, and unexpected expenses chip away at our budgets.

Frequently as money pressures mount, tensions arise and hostility erupts. Happy families become irritable and close ties are fequently severed by the sharp edge of the dollar bill.

But our troubles are really bigger than the bank balance or the budget—ours is a spiritual problem. Every difficulty is another opportunity. We can either trust God or trust ourselves.

Our unsaved neighbors know we are supposed to trust God. If we don't, we are proving to them

that we don't honestly believe that God will provide—even though we may have been telling them
for years that He does.

If we allow the cash conflict to build tension,
we are entering the danger zone. Quarreling families are noticed by the non-Christian. Once happy
families, that begin clawing at each other's throats
over an estate, broadcast their doubts that God
can deal fairly with them.

Pocketbook Perspective

Keeping our perspective about money is as difficult
as it is important. We can either be in charge of
our possessions or they will be in charge of us.
The choice is ours.

Abraham kept his possessions in perspective.
Since a feud was the last thing he wanted, he took
the initiative to cool the crisis before it reached
the boiling point. What began with verbal assaults
among the servants would soon build to something
more serious, unless action was taken.

Although it was within his rights to demand that
Lot's servants back down, Abraham approached
the matter wih extreme sensitivity. He said, "Please
let there be no strife between you and me, nor between my herdsmen and your herdsmen, for we
are brothers" (Gen. 13:8). He made a plea for
unity to preserve the harmony and their testimony
as worshipers of God in a pagan land.

Abraham had a plan. It must have startled Lot
when he said, "Is not the whole land before you?
Please separate from me: if to the left, then I will

go to the right; or if to the right, then I will go to the left" (Gen. 13:9). Abraham gave Lot first choice of grazing lands and placed his economic future on the line.

Abraham was a changed man. The experience in Egypt mellowed him and broadened his perspective. He was willing to trust God to provide for him from whatever was left over. Even though the food shortage was more critical than before and he was responsible for more people and livestock, Abraham was trusting God to care for his needs.

Children seldom learn from the mistakes of their parents and often repeat many of the same mistakes. Lot was that kind of person. His time in Egypt had not taught him anything. Abraham paid the price and learned the lesson, while Lot learned nothing.

Given the opportunity, Lot was perfectly willing to grasp what Abraham was giving up. He must have thought Abraham a fool for his offer, but he was not going to quibble with him about it. "Lot lifted up his eyes and saw all the valley of the Jordan that it was well watered everywhere" (Gen. 13:10). He lifted up his eyes to look, but only at the landscape. He had no thought of seeking direction from God.

As Lot surveyed the landscape, his major concern was financial. Since the valley was well watered, it would be ideal for his livestock. The cities of the plain must have reminded him of his recent trip to Egypt and the stories he had heard of Eden. In looking the situation over, Lot saw his opportunity for success. His herds would grow and a ready market was nearby in the cities. Besides, the bright lights and culture of Sodom would relieve the boredom of a herdsman's life.

"Lot chose for himself all the valley of the Jordan" (Gen. 13:11). Taking advantage of Abraham's generosity, he wasted no time in choosing. "Lot journeyed eastward . . . and settled in the cities of the valley, and moved his tents as far as Sodom" (Gen. 13:11-12). This move to Sodom was dictated by dollars. Lot was controlled by his wealth and the desire to preserve his money.

Abraham and Lot illustrate two different attitudes toward possessions. Some people trust God to supply their needs as He promised. They risk personal loss to preserve their Christian testimonies.

I know of one businessman who was promoted to a higher position with more pay and prestige. Before long, he realized the higher position took so much of his time that little was left to serve the Lord. He did the unthinkable. He went to his boss and asked for his old job so that he would have more time for the Lord's work. He was willing to be thought a fool by other believers so that he could serve the Lord—even though it meant a cut in pay.

Unfortunately, many Christians identify with Lot. Having become slaves to their pocketbooks, they can no longer rely on God. In the pursuit of the "title on the door and a carpet on the floor," they choose a location that enables them to ply their profession more lucratively.

Other Christians, when contemplating a move to a new location, spend long hours in extensive research. They write to the Chamber of Commerce seeking information on the schools, weather, water, and transportation offered by the community. But, like Lot, they ignore the spiritual climate and assume that all is well because most towns have churches.

Then there are those who attend the church of their choice, but keep a tight grip on the purse strings. They frequently complain, "They're always asking for money at church," without realizing that the grocer, the druggist, the gas station attendant and a host of others not only ask for money but demand it!

One day while talking to a businessman who had made his way to the top, I commented that rich people have it made. He immediately took issue with my oversimplification. He said, "The wealthy aren't free at all. They are slaves to their possessions, living in constant fear that something will happen to their things or that someone will sue them. They don't own their possessions, but rather are owned by them." The man spoke from first-hand experience about the enslaving bondage of greed.

After listening to him, it occurred to me that we should not envy the rich. Abraham's life would have been much easier had he not had so many servants and such vast livestock herds. Whether we have millions or nothing, we should be thankful to God.

Pocketbook Consequences

A coin has two sides—heads and tails. No matter how you flip the coin, it can only land on one side. Our decisions about money are like a coin toss. Our choices determine the consequences.

Abraham was blessed because he trusted God. He learned that he was not alone. Once Lot had packed his tent and moved to Sodom, God reminded Abraham that He was still with him.

God also reminded Abraham of His promises. The promise about the land was reiterated and expanded, as God told Abraham to look as far as he could see in every direction (Gen. 13:14-15). All that Abraham saw was promised to him and his descendents *forever*. As long as Lot was around, God did not give the land. But as soon as the separation was complete, God gave the title deed to Abraham.

Once he handed everything over to God, he was blessed. In gratitude, Abraham built his third altar to the Lord.

On the other hand, Lot experienced the agony of being a slave to money. He didn't consider the moral climate of the nearby cities when he chose Sodom. After all, what difference would it make to a herdsman? It may have been unimportant to Lot, but God wanted us to know about it. "The men of Sodom were wicked exceedingly and sinners against the Lord" (Gen. 13:13). Lot moved to "sin city" concerned only about his livestock.

He made a foolish decision in an effort to save his money. But he learned the tragic lesson that a fool and his money are soon parted. While living in Sodom he lost everything he tried to save and escaped only with the clothes on his back.

Lot probably hated himself for his greed in taking the "better" land for himself. He knew of Abraham's prosperity and peace as a nomad on the plains while his own money and possessions caused him much distress.

Sometimes we feel the same distress as Lot, when we find precious possessions becoming a burden. Instead of the luxury we had hoped for, we face the constant fear of losing what we have. The price of luxury is expensive—especially when it results in fear and worry.

In the final analysis, we know that it is better to trust God than to try our own home remedies. What Abraham was willing to give up, he was permitted to keep and was given more. What Lot tried to keep, he lost.

I have a brother who has a large successful machine shop, which specializes in aircraft landing gear repair. One day as we were visiting, I asked him how he had become so successful in such a short span of years. His story parallels the experience of Abraham and demonstrates that God *does* take care of His children who are willing to trust Him.

While working as a machinist for a large airline, my brother established a part-time machine shop business in his garage, with God as the Senior Partner. Night after night he worked in his garage. After a few years, he became successful and unconsciously decided he did not need God's help any longer. Almost overnight his business dropped off to nothing. For nearly a year the expensive machines sat idle.

Finally it dawned on him that his problem was caused by not allowing God to run his business. He wisely came back to God, confessed his sin, and reinstated God as the Senior Partner. It was only a short time before business was so good that he gave up his regular job and went into business with God full-time.

God continued to bless the shop and his efforts until he had to move out of the garage into a small building. Before long that small building was outgrown and a larger facility was built. Within a short time, that building was insufficient and another was built to accommodate the business.

The conclusion of his story tells why God had so blessed him. When his business was ready to double in capacity, he promised to give God a certain amount every week. Many Sunday mornings as he wrote his check, he had no idea where the money would come from to replace it. But each time God supplied it and gave more. He noticed that company sales had taken a sizeable jump every month since that date, and he was then preparing to increase the amount given to God.

When he finished with his story, he said, "I feel sorry for those Christians who are living on the crumbs. This is the only way to fly!"

He, like Abraham, learned that God can be trusted to supply our needs.

¹ And it came about in the days of Amraphel, king of Shinar, Arioch, king of Ellasar, Chedorlaomer, king of Elam, and Tidal, king of Goiim, ² that they made war with Bera, king of Sodom, and with Birsha, king of Gomorrah, Shinab, king of Admah, and Shemeber, king of Zeboiim, and the king of Bela (that is, Zoar). . . . Twelve years they had served Chedorlaomer, but the thirteenth year they rebelled. . . . ¹¹ Then they took all the goods of Sodom and Gomorrah and all their food supply, and departed. ¹² And they also took Lot, Abram's nephew. . . . ¹⁴ When Abram heard that his relative had been taken captive, . . . he led out his trained men, born in his house, three hundred and eighteen, and went in pursuit as far as Dan. . . . ¹⁶ And he brought back all the goods, and also brought back his relative Lot with his possessions, and also the women, and the people. . . . ¹⁷ The king of Sodom went out to meet him. . . . ¹⁸ And Melchizedek king of Salem brought out bread and wine; now he was a priest of God Most High. ¹⁹ And he blessed him. . . . ²⁰ And he [Abram] gave him a tenth of all. . . . ²² And Abram said to the king of Sodom . . . ²⁴ "I will take nothing. . . ." ¹⁵:¹ After these things the word of the Lord came to Abram. . . . ⁷ "I am the Lord who brought you out of Ur of the Chaldeans, to give you this land to possess it." ⁸ And he said, "O Lord God, how may I know that I shall possess it?" ⁹ So He said to him, "Bring Me a three-year-old heifer, and a three-year-old female goat, and a three-year-old ram, and a turtledove, and a young pigeon." ¹⁰ Then he brought all these to Him. . . . ¹⁷ And it came about when the sun had set, that it was very dark, and behold, there appeared a smoking oven and a flaming torch which passed between these pieces. ¹⁸ On that day the Lord made a covenant with Abram.

Genesis 14:1—15:18

4

The Peril of Success

When I was small, I frequently accompanied my dad when he took dull plowpoints to the blacksmith shop. I loved the smells and sounds of the shop and enjoyed watching the stooped smith at his work.

He put the plowpoint into his forge and pumped the bellows till the iron was red hot. Then he took it out, dipped it quickly into a vat of water, and while holding it on the anvil, he hammered away bringing the metal to a sharp edge.

Before going to the shop and seeing the blacksmith at work, I assumed that the plows were sharpened just by being taken to the shop. I had no idea what was involved in making the dull plowpoints sharp again. But one visit made me realize that producing a sharp point took heat, water, hammer, anvil, and the skill of a master smith applying the right pressure on the right spot at the right time.

Recalling that boyhood experience gives me a deeper understanding of one of the false assumptions we make about the Christian life. Since Christians are supposed to go to church, we unconsciously assume that church attendance provides all we need for a strong sharp faith.

However, it only takes a few trips into the shop of life to realize that great faith does not happen just by being around the shop. Faith grows strong only as it is heated in the forge of daily trials and hammered on the anvil of life by the Master Smith of the universe.

The Holy Spirit has captured in print the experiences of men whose faith was going through the sharpening process. One such man, Abraham, found his faith in the forge frequently. In his next encounter with God, we discover that one of the hammers used by God to sharpen our faith is success.

Faith and Success

Abraham's restful fellowship with God in Hebron was shattered by a new challenge—war erupted in the Jordan Valley. The five cities of the valley, ruled by the kings of Mesopotamia, had paid annual taxes for 12 years. In the thirteenth year they rebelled and in the fourteenth year a military expedition arrived to squelch the rebellion and restore the taxes.

In a fierce battle, the four invading kings overpowered the forces of the five kings. On vanquishing them, the victors "took all the goods of Sodom and Gomorrah and all their food supply . . . and they also took Lot, Abram's nephew, and his possessions and departed, for he was living in Sodom" (Gen. 14:11-12).

Lot's choice of the fertile valley had seemed like a good one. But now as the dust of battle cleared, Lot swallowed his first dose of the same medicine Abraham took in Egypt. He experienced the chastening hand of God as he lost his freedom and his possessions.

The news of the battle and Lot's capture was brought to Abraham by an escaped fugitive. This disquieting news issued a challenge to Abraham— what to do about Lot? He could ignore the problem. Adopting a "hands off" policy would make good sense since he and Lot were no longer partners. Or, he could adopt an attitude of self-righteous condemnation. After all, Lot was selfish when he chose the best for himself, so why bother about him now? "He's just getting what's coming to him." Or, as a third option, he could intervene in an attempt to rescue Lot from the invading kings.

Common sense argued against becoming involved. After all, it was not his fight and there was no point getting involved in someone else's scrape. Besides, Abraham was a dweller in tents, not a man of chariots; a wanderer on the plains of Canaan, not a warrior experienced in military campaigns. But the biggest argument against going to war was the risk. If he went against the kings and was defeated, he would lose everything.

Ignoring the dangers and risks involved, Abraham gave up his right to peace and went to war. "He led out his trained men, born in his house, three hundred and eighteen, and went in pursuit as far as Dan" (Gen. 14:14).

This decision gives us a glimpse into Abraham's heart, showing the value he placed on the life of a wayward nephew. His commitment to his family led him to risk everything for one man. Perhaps, from a human standpoint, Lot did not deserve this kind of commitment, but Abraham saw him as his responsibility, regardless of his character.

God honored his faith with a smashing victory. Facing overwhelming odds, the man of God became a man of war. Even though he had every reason to fear for his life, he led his band of men with boldness and confidence, pursuing the invaders. His men overcame them and pursued the stragglers before the battle ceased.

How was it that Abraham, who earlier had his wife lie to save his neck, was willing to face such overwhelming odds in battle? He was trusting God to keep His promise to make him into a great nation. No longer afraid, he went forth with almost reckless abandon—trusting God to turn the tide. In this new challenge Abraham allowed God to be God—doing what He promised to do.

Spiritual Warfare

We are all engaged in warfare. Our battles are spiritual not physical—the flesh against the spirit.

Paul described the warfare of the soul when he wrote: "For we naturally love to do evil things that are just the opposite from the things that the Holy Spirit tells us to do; and the good things we want to do when the Spirit has His way with us are just the opposite of our natural desires. These two forces within us are constantly fighting each other to win control over us and our wishes are never free from their pressures" (Gal. 5:17, LB).

Though this type of warfare is different than the physical war faced by Abraham, the principles are the same. The invading king of darkness seeks to overpower us, making us his slaves.

Christians are frequently taken captive by the evil desires that fight with our desire to do good. Self-serving choices, though apparently good, deliver us captive to our evil natures. The plight of Lot in the caravan, as a captive, illustrates the jams we may get ourselves into.

Every time a fellow Christian is in trouble, the rest of us are wearing Abraham's sandals. When we hear news of a brother's problems God places a new challenge of faith before us. We have the same options as Abraham did with Lot. Probably, most of us choose to ignore a brother's problems and walk by on the other side of the road. Others, unable to ignore the failure and sin of a brother, descend upon him with self-righteous indignation, agreeing that he deserves whatever he gets.

Unfortunately too few "good Samaritans" help the brother who is wounded and lies bleeding in the ditch. It could be because of the risks involved.

But each time a brother becomes a captive of sin and we know about it, we will exercise one option or the other.

Abraham's experience teaches us that we can trust God when we help a brother who is down. The New Testament hammers home our responsibilities to each other as members of God's family. Even though what our brother has done is terrible, we should not become self-righteous, for none is beyond going down to Sodom. We are just as vulnerable to failure as the one we are tempted to condemn. The temptation to condemn should be dulled by the reminder, "let him who thinks he stands take heed lest he fall" (1 Cor. 10:12).

Keeping our commitments to each other is not without risks. In helping a fallen brother back to his feet, we risk becoming a captive of the same desire. But when exercising loving concern for a brother, we don't back off just because it may cost us something.

Our obligation to lift up the fallen is clearly spelled out: "Dear brothers, if a Christian is overcome by some sin, you who are godly should gently and humbly help him back onto the right path, remembering that next time it might be one of you who is in the wrong. Share each other's troubles and problems, and so obey our Lord's command. If anyone thinks he is too great to stoop to this, he is fooling himself. He is really a nobody" (Gal. 6:1-3, lb). Since God has commanded that we help, we can trust Him when we seek to rescue brothers who are spiritual captives.

Whether the challenge is personal or not, Abraham teaches us that faith and success are inseparable. When we trust God, He enables us to successfully meet challenges according to His Word.

Faith for Success

Success ruins many good people in the business world. It also has the capability of ruining Christians who have been blessed by God. Once we trust God and exercise faith for success, that success presents a new challenge.

On returning from the defeat of the kings of the East, Abraham was met by two men—Melchizedek and the King of Sodom. The way in which he dealt with each man demonstrated how faith can survive the temptations of success.

Imagine the procession of the returning conqueror, bringing "all the goods, and also . . . his relative Lot with his possessions, and also the women and the people" (Gen. 14:16). He was a great hero.

In the encounter with Melchizedek, God received the glory for the success of Abraham. The king-priest of Salem (peace) met the returning warrior, bringing bread and wine for refreshment. What a different "coming home" than when he returned from Egypt. Then Abraham returned as a prodigal son, but now as a victorious warrior blessed by God.

Abraham also learned a new name for God, *El Elyon*. He had known God for some time, but now he discovered that the God he was serving was not just another god among the gods of the world but that He is "the Most High God." He also learned that God is the Creator of the heavens and the earth, and the God of battle. Abraham knew now why he was victorious over such overwhelming odds. It was the Most High God who delivered his enemies into his hands.

But the encounter with Melchizedek brought personal good news to Abraham. In the king-priest from Salem, he discovered a kindred spirit. During his stay in the land, Abraham had been alone, forced to depend on God without fellowship or outside counsel. But now God sent one with whom he could fellowship in the things of *El Elyon*. No doubt these two men learned a lot about God from sharing their common experiences of faith.

It also enabled him to overcome the urge to gloat in his victory. The Creator, God of the universe, delivered his enemies into his hands, so Abraham had no basis to pop his suspenders, thump his chest or take any credit.

Since it was God who protected him and gave the victory, "he gave Him a tenth of all" in recognition that everything had come from the hand of God. Giving a tenth to God was an act of worship, as Abraham acknowledged God's right to receive the glory. It was Abraham's way of saying, "To God be the glory, great things He has done."

The meeting with the King of Sodom presented another challenge—the temptation to make personal gain at another's expense. The King of Sodom became the original emcee of "Let's Make a Deal" when he said, "Give the people to me and take the goods for yourself" (Gen. 14:21).

What a temptation for a man who had earlier given in to the pull of the pocketbook. Here he had an opportunity to fatten his bankroll by adding the spoils of war to his holdings.

Abraham's response to the offer made it clear that he went forth to war only after consulting God. He told the king, "I have sworn to the Lord God Most High, Possessor of heaven and earth, that I will not take a thread or a sandal thong or anything that is yours . . . I will take nothing except what the young men have eaten and the share of the men who went with me" (Gen. 14:22-24).

It appears he had already made a better deal with God. He promised God that he would not make a profit at the expense of another's misery, if God would protect him. He and his men went forth with God on a nonprofit venture, requiring only that their expenses be paid.

But, we see his spiritual insight when he gave his reason for refusing even a sandal thong as payment, "lest you should say, I have made Abram rich." If God were to receive the glory, he made sure that no one else had the chance to horn in by suggesting that Abraham went to war for his personal profit.

It still takes faith to keep God-given success from ruining us. Because we are troubled by the evil desires of the flesh, we face a natural temptation to take credit for our successes.

If you listen carefully to a successful business-man, you will probably discover that he views his success as a result of his hard work and genius. Seldom do you hear a businessman, even a Christian, give God *all* the glory for his success. Some may mouth the words that God did it all, but underneath you sense they really don't believe that.

In our own personal ministries, we are tempted to think that success comes from our own insights and skills. If we trust God to do something through us, then He should get all the credit. If, on the other hand, we go out and do it on our own, don't try to force any glory or blame on Him!

Another truth which comes from this experience is that while we are giving the glory to God, we should also give Him some of our increase. When God blesses us above what we have now, in gratitude we likewise should "give Him a tenth of all." It is not because God needs our giving, but because we need to give to Him.

Every day we are faced with the chance to take credit for the good things that come our way. Only God can enable us to keep our success in perspective, thus making it possible for Him to bless us even more.

Faith and Rewards

God likes to give. He does not ask us to keep on giving to Him with the prospect of receiving nothing in return. Abraham discovered that God rewarded him for his trust. Perhaps after Abraham had refused to make a profit he began to have second thoughts about the whole venture. It was "after these things the Word of the Lord came" (Gen. 15:1), revealing that God takes care of His own.

After all the excitement had died down and Abraham returned to his camp, he probably felt uneasy as fear of a reprisal raid gripped his soul. It had been a bold stroke for him to encounter and overpower the four eastern kings, taking their spoil. Now, when the time for war came again it was likely these men would come looking for "Abraham the Hebrew" (Gen. 14:13).

God said, "Do not fear . . . I am a shield to you" (Gen. 15:1). He was assured that the God who whipped them in the first place would protect him against any reprisal. He knew that his life was safe because God could be depended on.

God also reminded him of the promises when He said "Your reward shall be very great" (Gen. 15:1). Abraham, who was advanced in years, had been believing that God would give him children. But perhaps he had begun to doubt just a little. If God's reward was going to be so great, why was it that he had no children? Furthermore, what was the point of making him so great since a hired servant would be his heir?

In response to his questions, God reaffirmed the promise of children. God said that the servant would not inherit all his holdings. Then Abraham was invited to count the stars of the sky. Realizing the impossibility of that, Abraham was told that his seed would be as numerous as the stars.

When such an announcement was made, we read some of the most profound and yet most simple words in all Scripture, "Then he believed in the Lord, and He reckoned it to him as righteousness" (Gen. 15:6).

God reaffirmed the fact that Abraham's descendants would indeed possess the land. For almost a decade Abraham had followed God around the landscape, believing some tall promises. Finally, he got up his courage and asked God if He would mind putting the promises in writing. "How may I know that I shall possess it?" (Gen. 15:8)

It was then that God bound himself unconditionally to Abraham by making a blood covenant. He was instructed to prepare certain animals for sacrifice. When Abraham fell asleep, God passed between the sacrificial animals reciting the terms of the contract (Gen. 15:18).

We know that God cares for us. We may pass up the career opportunity of a lifetime, and in the days following, face the gnawing question of whether we did the right thing. It is then we need to listen to the still small voice inside which says, "I'll take care of you."

We never have to fear being left out and alone. Jesus promised, "I am with you always" (Matt. 28:20). Even in times when it seems that we have been utterly forsaken by everyone, even God, we need to listen to God's voice of friendship and comfort.

When we consider some of the great things God

has promised us, we might wonder about His reliability. Unlike Abraham, we have never had to walk with God on His oral promises alone. All His promises are in writing and have been guaranteed by a blood covenant. When Jesus hung between heaven and earth, He was signing our contract with God.

Think about some of the things Jesus said at the Last Supper. Lifting the cup, He said, "This cup . . . is the New Covenant in My blood" (Luke 22:20). The covenant between Abraham and God was sealed by the blood of animals, but the New Covenant of life has been sealed by the precious blood of Christ. Indeed, in Him our reward shall be exceedingly great.

God, the Master Smith of the universe, frequently places our faith in His forge and heats it by trials. When the metal of our faith is hot, He lays it on the anvil of life and expertly hammers it to a sharp edge. Without His master touch in the hour of trials our faith would never develop sharpness.

Regardless of the challenge, we can place it before God, trusting Him for the ability to overcome the problem. And then we can say, "To God be the glory, great things He has done."

What challenge of faith are you facing? Abraham's story teaches that you can commit the challenge to God completely, being confident that He will work through any problem in your life. The only question you must answer is: Will you allow Him to be the God of trials in your life?

¹ Now Sarai, Abram's wife had borne him no children. . . . So Sarai ² said to Abram, ". . . Please go in to my maid; perhaps I shall obtain children through her." . . . ⁴ And he went in to Hagar, and she conceived; and . . . her mistress was despised in her sight. . . . ⁶ So Sarai treated her harshly, and she fled from her presence. . . . ⁹ Then the angel of the Lord said to her, "Return to your mistress, and submit yourself to her authority." . . . ¹⁶ And Abram was eighty-six years old when Hagar bore Ishmael to him. ¹⁷:¹ Now when Abram was ninety-nine years old, the Lord appeared to Abram and said to him, . . . ⁵ "No longer shall your name be called Abram, but your name shall be Abraham; for I will make you the father of a multitude of nations. . . . ¹⁰ This is My covenant, which you shall keep, between Me and you and your descendants after you: every male among you shall be circumcised. . . . ¹⁵ As for Sarai your wife, you shall not call her name Sarai, but Sarah shall be her name. ¹⁶ And I will bless her, and indeed I will give you a son by her. . . ." ¹⁷ Then Abraham fell on his face and laughed. . . . ¹⁸ And Abraham said to God, "Oh that Ishmael might live before Thee!" ¹⁹ But God said, ". . . He shall become the father of twelve princes, and I will make him a great nation. ²¹ But My covenant I will establish with Isaac. . . ." ²⁴ Now Abraham was ninety-nine years old when he was circumcised in the flesh of his foreskin.   Genesis 16:1—17:24

5

Hurry Up and Wait

Hurry up and wait!

Many people use that expression in describing their time in military service. It seems that the military wants you to hurry everywhere you go—then stand around waiting once there.

I know from personal experience that a man in the military spends a great deal of time hurrying. In basic training we were rousted out of bed early and rushed down to the chowhall where we stood in line half an hour before breakfast; marched double time to the dispensary where we stood in line waiting for shots; and rushed to the air terminal only to stand around waiting for the flight to arrive. Nothing ever was ready when we were ready for it, so we learned to wait.

Life in general is a waiting game. Few stop to realize just how much of our lives is spent waiting for something to happen. We wait for the car to be fixed; for dinner to cook; for pay day to come. The expression "a watched pot never boils" reminds us that consciously waiting for something makes time drag.

Even Christians are plagued by the problem of waiting. It's uncanny how often we are expected to wait patiently on the Lord. It seems as though God wants us to hurry up so we can sit and wait for Him to act.

Our impatience with God is not new. Men of faith have always experienced the frustration of waiting for God. In examining the life of Abraham, we discover in his fifth encounter with God that he played the waiting game.

Waiting Breeds Impatience

Waiting is one of the most difficult assignments in life, especially when we don't know how long we must wait. The longer we wait, the more likely we are to find impatience gnawing on our faith. Abraham, though he had had revelation of God's will for his life, began to feel the pressure of impatience.

God's promise of children to Abraham became a point of testing. Three times God promised that His will for Abraham included children as the "dust of the earth" and the stars of the heavens, but 10 years elapsed and "Sarai, Abram's wife, had borne him no children" (Gen. 16:1).

After 10 years, each month that passed made it more doubtful that God would keep His promise.

The advanced ages of Abraham and Sarah (he was 85 and she 75) increased the anxiety. Each day the promise did not come to pass gave rise to a very practical question: Would God keep His promise to bless Abraham with children?

The frustration of waiting on God was wearing on his soul. Of course, Abraham could keep on waiting, even though time was running out. Or he could completely give up any idea of ever having a son. But God's promise had given him hope, and that hope was hard to abandon now. So he quit waiting for God and did something about the problem himself.

Actually Sarah came up with the idea first. She said, "Now behold, the Lord has prevented me from bearing children. Please go in to my maid; perhaps I shall obtain children through her" (Gen. 16:2).

Sarah honestly did not believe that God would give her children. She knew the hurt Abraham felt from this lack. So in an act of sacrificial love, she offered to share her husband with Hagar so that he could become a father.

Although this idea sounds crude, it was consistent with the customs then. Other men did it, and the offspring of the servant was called the child of the wife. Surely Abraham realized that God's promise said nothing about Sarah. Since time *was* running out, this looked like the only plan that would work.

Like a good husband, he "listened to the voice of Sarai . . . and he went in to Hagar and she conceived" (Gen. 16:2-4). Immediately Abraham became an expectant father and his hopes of having children were rekindled. It looked like his lifelong dream would be fulfilled.

But all was not as well as it seemed. Abraham was *so* anxious to have a son that he acted without consulting God. Earlier he had gone to Egypt without consulting God and returned with a maid named Hagar. Now Hagar was being used in an attempt to fulfill God's promise.

Abraham's tent filled with tension. "When she saw that she had conceived, her mistress was despised in her sight" (Gen. 16:4). Having two women under the same tent produced a lot of friction. Abraham's hopes were shattered when Hagar, tired of Sarah's abuse, ran away.

Abraham's impatient action gave birth to the Arab people. The prophecy concerning the son of this union, that he should dwell in defiance of all his brothers (Gen. 16:12), has been documented in blood and trouble. What seemed so logical was really an attempt to get God out of a tight spot.

Abraham believed God was going to give him a son, but he was impatient with God's timing. When waiting got too tough, he decided God needed a little help.

His experience rings a bell. Even though God has revealed much of His will in the Bible, certain areas of life require waiting for more direction. We have no problem in glibly saying "My God shall supply your every need," and "God won't permit any temptation to become too great," and "It isn't His will that any should perish." But once the words have slipped out, the real struggle begins—waiting for God to do what He promised.

Lending God a Hand

When we promise a child something, he wants it right away, and will drive a parent to distraction until he gets it or gives up in disgust. Most of us are like small children, wanting God to fulfill every promise the instant we ask. We want God to be our heavenly bellhop. When He doesn't answer immediately, we keep pressing the button or else give up in frustration.

We get tired of praying for an unsaved relative year after year; or praying the old car will keep running; or trusting God for the money for our children's braces.

When it looks like God won't come through, we get edgy. We unconsciously decide that God must need our help, so we plan to solve our own problems. We begin to use "strong-arm evangelism" with the unsaved relative; trade in the old car while it still runs; or borrow on the insurance policy to get the kids' braces. These actions are logical to us, and they seem to work. Besides, God has not condemned us, so it must be okay with Him.

When our church was planning to expand, one board member said, "God knows that we need an architect. So let's claim His promise to supply our needs." We began to pray, but when no architect appeared, we hired a draftsman. He drew the floor plan three times and each time it was wrong. He did not give us what we wanted. Finally, God had mercy on us and provided His architect, who was eager to use his training for God. But our problems came because we did not really believe God, so we tried our own plan.

I have friends who have shared Abraham's experience. They discovered God's will for them included training in Bible school. They were so enthused that they immediately sold their house, moved to another city and enrolled in classes. Within two months they both flunked out. We could not understand why God led them there and abandoned them. But after they returned, we learned the whole story. They knew God wanted them in Bible school, but they did not know *when*. In their anxiety to do God's will, they left town and some unfinished tasks to go to school. They experienced the heartbreak of failure because they did not wait for God's timing.

God's Stubborn Love

We frequently give up on other people when they disappoint us. But God is not like that. His stubborn love and grace refuse to give up on any of us, no matter how often we disappoint Him.

God was gracious to a man who was grasping at straws. In spite of Abraham's impatience, and after a silence of 14 years, "When Abram was ninety-nine years old, the Lord appeared to Abram" (17:1). For 13 years a doting old father lived with his own remedy, ignorant that his plan was not going to work.

Before God broke the news to Abraham concerning the folly of his own plan, He prepared him with new revelation. He told him that He is *El Shaddai,* the Almighty God, and that He would multiply him exceedingly.

Next, Abraham received news concerning himself. For 99 years he had been called Abram, which meant "high father," but now God was changing his name to Abraham—"father of a multitude." Also Sarai, which meant "contentious," would be changed to Sarah—"princess." Abraham then learned that his plan was wrong. God said, "I will bless her (Sarah), and indeed I will give you a son by her" (Gen. 17:16).

Abraham's response was normal. He "fell on his face and laughed and said in his heart, 'Will a child be born to a man one hundred years old? And will Sarah, who is ninety years old bear a child?'" (Gen. 17:17) He did not believe that God could do it. The suggestion was preposterous.

Anyway, he already had a son. Since he and Sarah were both too old to bear children, he pleaded with God for Ishmael. He had dreamed that the boy was the promised child. Now it was hard to face reality, even though God's plan did not include a covenant relationship with Ishmael. He would bless Ishmael, but the covenant would be established with Sarah's son—Isaac.

Why would God deny an old man his request? Because Ishmael was the product of impatience—

a natural solution to a supernatural problem. God had promised a son, but Abraham relied on his own plan. Ishmael was not the son of promise, so he was rejected by God.

Abraham also forgot about God's timing. God deliberately waited until he and Sarah were beyond childbearing years to reveal His plan. Facing the impossible, Abraham was now expected to trust the Almighty God. Earlier, he asked God for proof that he would fulfill His promise. Now God asked Abraham to prove that he believed. Circumcision was the visible sign to God that Abraham and his descendants believed Him.

In longsuffering and grace, God did not turn Abraham aside. He continued to bless and love him until he realized that God could do the impossible. Once he understood this, Abraham circumcised all the males in his camp as a sign that he believed *El Shaddai.*

It is comforting to read about God's stubborn love toward a man who became impatient with Him. God does not become impatient with His impatient children. Part of His plan may be to allow us to wallow in our own solutions. When we have experienced the anxiety of trying to do God's work our way, it is easier to accept His plan.

But there is one costly result. We lose precious time that could have been used for God. It's like missing a turn on the freeway because we were not paying attention. Eventually, we will discover our mistake and backtrack for miles before we find the right road.

God's Perfect Timing

God's tender love and promises are not withdrawn because we don't trust Him and His timing for our lives. He hangs on and waits until we are ready to play His way—then He blesses us by grace.

God's timing is always perfect. It is hard to understand why we must wait so long for an unsaved relative to come to Christ, or for a particular need to be met. Perhaps we need to learn the valuable lesson of trusting God. When we *do* wait and see God work, our confidence in His ability grows.

We must remember that we are trusting *El Shaddai*, the Almighty God. He has never made a promise He is unable to fulfill. We have all seen someone who seemed beyond God's reach. Yet, in God's perfect timing, the hard heart was broken and the unbeliever turned to Christ.

We also must remember the long-range consequences of our own remedies. What Abraham did seemed insignificant, yet it gave rise to centuries of animosity and warfare between the sons of Isaac and the sons of Ishmael. Even though we may recover from the error of our decisions, the long-range results of an impatient act can be devastating.

When we act without God, we make as much sense as a man who hits himself on the thumbnail with a hammer to relieve a headache. A lot of frustration and trouble could be eliminated if we would wait *patiently* for God.

A friend told me of his struggle in trusting God

for his father's salvation. As a young man, he came to Christ and as a new Christian became concerned about his dad. He and others began to pray that his dad would come to Christ. As his father grew older, the son felt that time was running out. Anxious to see his father believe, he began to get pushy. But his father grew more resistant. Finally he backed off and started to wait again. As his dad advanced further in years, the son was even more concerned about his salvation.

Finally, one evening the telephone rang. His dad called because he had just trusted Christ as his Saviour and wanted him to know. His son had prayed, sometimes impatiently, for 29 years—waiting for the news.

How long should we wait for God to fulfill His promise? For 29 years or however long it may take. It is better to wait, than to act and then regret it.

[1] Now the Lord appeared to him by the oaks of Mamre. . . . [2] Three men were standing opposite him; and when he saw them, he . . . [3] said, "My lord, if now I have found favor in your sight, please do not pass your servant by." . . . [9] They said to him . . . [10] "Sarah your wife shall have a son." . . . [12] And Sarah laughed to herself, saying, "After I have become old, shall I have pleasure, my lord being old also?" . . . [14] "Is anything too difficult for the Lord? At the appointed time I will return to you." . . . [20] And the Lord said, "The outcry of Sodom and Gomorrah is indeed great." . . . [23] And Abraham came near and said, "Wilt Thou indeed sweep away the righteous with the wicked?" . . . [32] And He said, "I will not destroy it on account of the ten." [19:1] Now the two angels came to Sodom. . . . [15] And when morning dawned, the angels urged Lot. . . . [16] But he hesitated. So the men seized his hand and the hand of his wife and the hands of his daughters, for the compassion of the Lord was upon him; and they brought him out, and put him outside the city. . . . [17] One said, "Escape for your life! Do not look behind you, and do not stay anywhere in the valley." . . . [24] Then the Lord rained on Sodom and Gomorrah brimstone and fire. . . . [26] But his wife, from behind him, looked back; and she became a pillar of salt. . . . [29] God remembered Abraham, and sent Lot out of the midst of the overthrow.   Genesis 18:1—19:29

6

A Pile of Ashes

One of the great classics of college football is the gridiron clash between the University of Texas and Texas A & M. This annual battle captures the interest of football fans throughout the great southwest.

But each year before the game, a moving human drama little known to the public is enacted by the cadets of Texas A & M. For weeks prior to the game, the cadets spend long hours getting ready for the pep rally. They cut and haul trees to the campus, where they are added to the wood prepared for the gigantic bonfire.

When the proper moment arrives, the huge pile is ignited and flames race toward the sky. By the time that night is over, all that remains is a pile of smoldering ashes—all their labor gone up in smoke.

I have often wondered how the cadets feel as they work like slaves building something to be burned. To some it must seem like an exercise in futility. But to others, the effort expended is worthwhile because of the joy in doing the assigned task.

We may joke about the burnt enthusiasm of the cadets, but it should be an example to us. Have you ever considered that you may be spending long hours piling up fuel for a gigantic spiritual bonfire? The Bible teaches it and Abraham experienced it.

Faith in the Furnace

God does not allow us to be under pressure all the time. No one can stand constant stress on his faith without cracking. Periods of rest and peace are essential to maintain sanity.

Abraham was prepared for a new trial of his faith by a period of rest and fellowship with God. The Lord appeared with two angels in the form of men. Abraham begged the pleasure of their fellowship. He hurried from the tent and hasty preparations were begun for a meal which he shared with the Lord and the two angels.

God also gave Abraham new words of encouragement concerning the promised son. Some things need to be said over and over again before we really believe them. Abraham had heard repeatedly that he would have a son, but at last he was told, "At this time next year . . . Sarah your wife shall have a son . . ." (Gen. 18:10). She had been in the background, but now knowing it was physically impossible for her to bear children, she laughed to herself (Gen. 18:12).

God reassured them with a question: "Is anything too difficult for the Lord?" The Almighty God specializes in doing what is humanly impossible. Naturally, Sarah denied her laughter, but had been caught in the act of unbelief just as Abraham had earlier.

Having fellowshiped with God and received encouragement, he was now ready for the next test. As the three visitors prepared to depart, the Lord said, " Shall I hide from Abraham what I am about to do?" (Gen. 18:17) Since Abraham was personally involved in what would happen, there was no need to keep him in the dark.

The reason for the journey was to investigate the state of affairs in Sodom (Gen. 18:20-21). The Lord's visit brought good news and bad news, which Abraham received with mixed emotions. The good news of his son's birth probably quickened his pulse. However, the good was tempered by the word of the visit to Sodom.

That information presented another challenge of faith for Abraham. He was a practical man, and a realist. He knew what conditions God would find in Sodom. He also knew that total destruction was warranted.

Abraham's sense of fairness surfaced as he pleaded with God for Sodom's deliverance, based on the presence of the good people who lived there. He appealed to God's integrity: "Shall not the Judge of the earth deal justly?" (Gen. 18:25)

When informed that God would spare the city for 50 righteous people, Abraham continued to lower the number until he reached 10.

Fire for Sodom

Why was Abraham so concerned about Sodom? First, because Lot, his only blood relative nearby, was living there. But that does not explain his urgent anxiety. If that were his only concern, he could have asked God to get Lot out before He judged Sodom.

Secondly, Abraham risked a great deal to rescue the people of Sodom when they were captives. In practical terms, he might be called the "patron saint" of the city. Everyone knew that Abraham was responsible for the restoration of Sodom.

Finally, the cities of the plain were a visible testimony to God's power. Abraham's army was outmanned and outgunned, yet God gave them the victory. God, not Abraham, had defeated the kings, and the deliverance of the people was evidence of God's might.

It just did not make sense that God would enable him to rescue and restore the cities so He could later destroy them for their sin. Abraham could logically reason, "I wasted my time and risked my life serving God when I went to war, and now it will go up in smoke." The temptation was to view the war as an exercise in futility. Why should Abraham bother to work and trust the Lord, when He would just burn up the results?

Abraham's experience is an excellent object lesson for us, since we face the same temptation today. It would be one thing, if we did not know that some of our work for Christ will be burned. But God does not keep us in the dark. He has let us in on His plans. "I no longer call you slaves, for a master doesn't confide in his slaves; now you are My friends, proved by the fact that I have told you everything the Father told Me" (John 15:15, LB).

God will summon us to stand before the Judgment Seat of Christ for the purpose of examining what we did for Him during our lives. The picture is that of having our works pass through a refining fire. Some of our deeds can be compared to precious metals which survive the refiner's fire, but others, like wood, hay, and stubble, will be reduced to ashes.

Realizing that much of our work may go up in smoke produces a practical test of faith. Some Christians, considering that they may be doing some things that will not pass the test, suffer from the "paralysis of analysis." So much time is spent fretting about motives that little or nothing is done for God.

Others become angry with God and claim He is unfair. We may say, "After all, I'm doing the best I can for the Lord. What more does He expect? How can I be expected to work hard with the threat hanging over my head that it won't last anyway?"

We may even be tempted to sit down and do

nothing for God. After all if we don't do anything for Him, He can't burn anything up. What a sly one Satan is if he gets you to bite that hook.

The whole issue of the trial of our works is a test of faith. A realization that God may enable us to do a particular service for Him, and then burn it up because our motives were impure, is serious business. The trial by fire is a real test to faith in action. How can we face the possibility of loss and yet go on?

Grace to Endure

The grace of God keeps us serving Him even when we do not understand how He works. An examination of the situation at Sodom reveals that His grace to go on is bestowed upon the good and the not-so-good.

Abraham was still learning to trust God for everything. When he stopped interceding for Sodom, he committed the matter to God. Abraham was assured that God would not destroy the good with the bad (Gen. 18:26). God could be trusted to make the right decision concerning the people of Sodom.

God also demonstrated His faithfulness to Abraham. "God remembered Abraham, and sent Lot out of the midst of the overthrow" (Gen. 19:29). When news of Lot's deliverance reached Abraham, he realized that God did not destroy a single righteous soul with the wicked of the city.

Lot, though living in Sodom, received an abundant measure of God's grace, even though he did not deserve it. The war and captivity had not taught Lot or the other men of Sodom anything. Shortly after the war, they had settled down in their old ways again.

Lot was so blinded by love for his possessions that he even resisted God's grace. He was told of the impending destruction of Sodom and urged to take his wife and two daughters, and leave town. If he stayed, certain destruction would engulf him, but he was in no hurry to give up his holdings in Sodom.

Once the angels "seized his hand . . . and brought him out, and put him outside the city" (Gen. 19:16), he still resisted the grace of God. When told to head for the hills to escape judgment, he did not want to go. It took the firm hand of God to pry Lot loose so his life could be spared.

In the midst of the trial, Lot was disciplined for his backsliding. Living in Sodom cost him his testimony. When he tried to restrain the men of Sodom, they replied, "This one came in as an alien, and already he is acting like a judge" (Gen. 19:9). The man of God lost his credibility while living in Sodom.

He also lost his possessions. His earlier decision to move to Sodom came from his desire for wealth. But now after living in the city and possibly accumulating more wealth and status, he lost everything and escaped from Sodom wearing only the clothes on his back.

But he lost something more precious—his wife. She, being no more anxious than Lot to leave everything behind, turned to look back. This was her last time to disobey God. They were told to move ahead and not look back. The instant she turned and looked, she became a pillar of salt (Gen. 19:26).

Losing his testimony, his possessions, and his wife may seem like hard discipline, but it was necessary to prepare him to appreciate the grace of God. Even though he had fled with nothing, he was alive and breathing, while all his neighbors and his wife were dead. God also was gracious in allowing him to choose his own way, granting his request to live in Zoar.

Perhaps the sweetest token of grace to Lot was what his presence meant to the inhabitants of Sodom. The people deserved instant destruction, but the angel, in urging him to hurry, said, "I cannot do anything until you arrive there" (Gen. 19:22). Had Lot not been there, perhaps God's fiery destruction would have fallen earlier.

God's grace is not limited only to those who follow in God's ways. In Abraham and Lot, we find one who served God and one who did not. But God made no distinction—He gave grace to both men.

The same God still gives us grace to continue serving Him, even though we know that much of what we do will not get by the fire. It is frustrating that some of our work for the Lord may be an exercise in futility. We may sing, teach, and serve, only to discover that at times our motives were less than pure, causing such service to go up in smoke. In the process of serving Him, we may in fact lose some things that are very precious to us, which will tempt us to give up and persevere no longer.

God continues to give us grace to go on. Even though I may not receive an immediate reward for some service to Him, those who received the service were blessed by God in the process. In that sense what is done, though not a blessing to me, does bring encouragement to someone else.

Even when we are wrapped up in our own activities and resist His gracious offerings, God reaches out to us. When we become lazy and refuse to serve Him, He still gives. Some will appear before the Judgment Seat and see every last thing they have done go up in smoke, but in grace, they will be saved, but "so as through fire" (1 Cor. 3:15).

Living Lessons
Interwoven in the story about the destruction of Sodom and Gomorrah are four eternal principles that strengthen our faith.

1. The value of intercession. Few men have shown the same degree of persistence in interceding on the behalf of others as Abraham. Through the process of interceding, he never lost sight of God's holiness. But he discovered that intercession has a limit, a point beyond which it is useless to plead with God.

Perhaps the greatest lesson in intercession is what it teaches us about God. Unfortunately we usually think about what we can receive by intercession. But what we learn about God in the process of intercession is more important than what we receive from Him.

2. The power of sin to enslave us. As in Lot's case, our circumstances have a powerful hold on us. We may have our own "Sodom" which God wants us to give up, but we hesitate because it is more precious to us than God is.

3. The worth of Christians in the world. Living in a godless society subjects us to verbal abuses and put-downs. It does not take too much of that kind of treatment to make us feel worthless. But the world owes us a lot more than they know.

The presence of the Holy Spirit as a restrainer of evil purifies the world (2 Thes. 2:7). If people think life is bad now, just wait till the Spirit is removed and sin is unrestrained.

In addition, our presence postpones God's judgment of the world. We know that God will judge the world with fire, just as He did Sodom and Gomorrah. But as the presence of Lot in the cities delayed the fiery hand of God, so also His judgment on the world will be delayed till all the Christians are safely out.

4. The service we owe to God. God is not interested in lining eternity with monuments to our honor. Work we do with that unconscious motive in mind will be consigned to the fire. We're all human and sometimes our humanity hinders our Christian service. God will judge all our works through the unobscured lens of holiness. When He sees work done for our own glory, He will burn it. We may be tempted to stop standing on the promises and start sitting on the premises. However, God's grace is given to keep us faithful, facing life with His power.

A pastor related a dream that illustrates the point well. He dreamed that the time had come for him to stand before the Judgment Seat of Christ. As he stood there, a door opened on one side of the room and an angel came in and piled up everything that he had done for the Lord during his entire life. The pile looked impressive, reaching almost to the ceiling. Then another angel came in with a match that he set at the bottom of the pile.

For a few minutes the fire burned furiously. Finally, when the fire died, another angel entered with a dustpan and broom. He bent over and swept up what was left of the huge stack—three nuggets of gold and a few ashes.

With that he awoke with a start. Struck by the fact that most of what he was doing could be burned at the Judgment Seat of Christ, he asked God to give him grace to do everything for His glory.

What will happen when all that you have done is tried by the fire of God? Will it endure as precious metals or will it be reduced to a pile of ashes?

[1] Now it came about after these things, that God tested Abraham. . . . [2] And He said, "Take now your son, your only son, whom you love, Isaac, and go to the land of Moriah; and offer him there as a burnt offering. . . ." [3] So Abraham rose early in the morning, . . . [6] took the wood of the burnt offering and laid it on Isaac his son, and he took in his hand the fire and the knife. So the two of them walked on together. [7] And Isaac spoke . . . "Behold, the fire and the wood, but where is the lamb for the burnt offering?" [8] And Abraham said, "God will provide for Himself the lamb for the burnt offering, my son." . . . [9] Then they came to the place of which God had told him; and Abraham built the altar there, and arranged the wood, and bound his son Isaac, and laid him on the altar on top of the wood. [10] And Abraham stretched out his hand, and took the knife to slay his son. [11] But the angel of the Lord called, . . . [12] "Do not stretch out your hand against the lad, and do nothing to him; for now I know that you fear God, since you have not withheld your son, your only son from Me." [13] Then Abraham raised his eyes and looked, and behold, behind him a ram caught in the thicket by his horns; and Abraham . . . offered him up . . . in the place of his son. [14] And Abraham called the . . . place The Lord Will Provide. . . . [15] Then the angel of the Lord called, . . . [16] "Because you have . . . not withheld your son . . . [17] indeed I will greatly bless you. . . ." [19] So Abraham returned to his young men, and they arose and went together to Beersheba; and Abraham lived at Beersheba.

Genesis 22:1-19

Journey Through Loneliness

Personal commitment is never easy. That basic fact of life needs to be permanently etched into the mind of every Christian. Somehow we assume that we will ultimately reach the point where it is easy to make commitments to God. We hope to grow beyond the inner struggle.

When I was a young Christian, I went through periods of inner struggle when faced with the decision of giving God control of various areas of my life. While facing the agony of inner decisions, I envied some of the "older" Christians who seemed able to commit new areas of their lives to God without any great difficulties. Secretly, I longed for the day when I, too, would arrive at that level of maturity.

I now realize no one ever becomes so mature that personal commitments come without a struggle.

For the more we grow, the greater are the commitments God asks us to make.

This used to bother me until I discovered a man who had walked with God for many years was going through the same struggles which confront every Christian. On the surface, Abraham's offering of Isaac on Mount Moriah seems a victory for those who claim deep commitments to God come easily to the mature.

However, don't be too quick to accept that conclusion. In our treatment of the offering of Isaac, we usually ignore the human struggles in the interest of getting on to the important matter of the substitution of the ram for Isaac.

But, when we view the experience of Abraham from his perspective, we get a different feeling. Looking at it through his eyes we can learn several important things about personal commitment.

Journey into Loneliness

The decision to commit things to God has never been easy, often coming only after a lonely struggle within the soul. We have seen glimpses of this struggle in the life of Abraham as he faced various tests of his faith. Some tests seemed rather severe, but the hardest came when God said, "Take now your son . . . and offer him there as a burnt offering . . ." (Gen. 22:2).

The intensely personal nature of this test is underscored by the words, "your son, your only son, whom you love" (Gen. 22:2). As the words echoed in his mind, God touched the most sensitive nerve of his soul. He had waited for Isaac for 25 years. He had given up his hopes for Ishmael and pinned all his hopes for the fulfillment of God's promises on Isaac. But as he neared the end of life, God asked him to take his most precious treasure, Isaac, who was more dear to him than life itself, and place him on an altar as a sacrifice.

The decision to follow God was the hardest one Abraham ever made and came only after a deep personal struggle. I doubt that he slept very much, for during the night he wrestled with many questions. Perhaps he asked himself, "Why this?" He had land, livestock, and money he could give. Why did God want him to offer Isaac? What would happen to God's promises about the great nation if he plunged the knife into Isaac? God told Abraham that Isaac would carry on the line and father a great multitude, but dead men sire no sons.

Perhaps an even more basic question tormented him: "Why did God give me Isaac and let me love him for so long and now want him back?" The decision to surrender something very precious is never easy and Abraham had no one to consult. He was totally alone.

That night of questioning found no answer. But God's question was: "Abraham, do you love Me more than Isaac, or is he the most important object of your devotion?" That was the real issue. What was number one in Abraham's life—God or Isaac?

With light beginning to dawn, Abraham made his choice. He "rose early in the morning and saddled his donkey, and took two of his young men with him and Isaac his son; and he split wood for the burnt offering, and arose and went to the place of which God had told him" (Gen. 22:3).

The decision to obey God took on a fatal air as four men left Beersheba for Moriah—a journey Abraham had no desire to take. For Abraham it was a journey into loneliness.

The young men traveling with them did not know the heaviness of the father's heart. Isaac, walking with Abraham, did not suspect Abraham's oppressive loneliness as they neared the place of sacrifice. Innocently he asked, "Behold, the fire and the wood, but where is the lamb for the burnt offering?" (Gen. 22:7) Imagine the hurt that coursed through Abraham's heart with his son's question. How could he tell Isaac that *he* was what God required?

Though not completely understanding how, Abraham expressed confidence that God *would* provide. Having tied his son and placed him on the altar, Abraham surrendered to God as he raised the knife to kill his beloved Isaac. In an instant he would give back to God what he had waited so long for and had enjoyed so much. Abraham made his greatest commitment to God—a lonely commitment.

The Struggle of Sacrifice

We can identify with his deep personal struggle, for we are asked to make our own lonely trips to Moriah. We too form deep and close attachments to the treasures and pleasures of life. Some value their children as their most prized possessions. To others, success becomes the object of worship. Others cherish their reputations more than aything else. Still others become attached to their personal fortunes.

Some objects of our affection may be good. But if we let them become paramount in our lives, we will hear God's voice asking us to put Him first instead.

God's call to commitment may mean sending the cherished son to a faraway mission field; or giving up the promising career to serve the Lord; or releasing the grip on a terminally ill loved one; or entrusting your reputation to God.

Whatever the test, it will ultimately involve what you love more than anything else in the world. God may ask you to place it on the altar and walk away if necessary, trusting Him to provide and compensate for the emptiness and loneliness that follows. We will never be able to do this without the gnawing question—WHY? But God will also be asking a question: "Do you love Me more than your career, your children, or your reputation?" Your answer will tell Him what is number one in your life.

Few make deep personal commitments without a fierce inner struggle. When we do struggle and wonder why, we may feel guilty for questioning God at all. But it is not unspiritual to ask Why. A parent would think it strange if a child never asked Why? when told to do some things. God, in His relationship to us as a Father, does not expect us to respond to His requests with blind obedience, never asking Why. When God asks us to give up things that are precious, He is not surprised if we wonder why.

Few, if any of our friends, understand the turmoil we feel when faced with a commitment to God. They cannot know or appreciate the vacuum that comes when God asks us to give up a job, a child, or a home. Our personal struggles are journeys into loneliness.

We may make our commitments without having any answers from God. But when we raise the knife to plunge it into our most prized possession, then we begin to get the answers.

Making our commitment is like entering a tunnel. It may seem dark, but once we reach the midway point, we see the light from the other end. The road that leads *into* the loneliness also leads *out*.

Journey out of Loneliness

When Abraham placed everything on the line for God, he began to emerge from his loneliness. Having gone to the brink with God, he felt the joy of being liberated from the loneliness that gnawed his soul during the journey to Mount Moriah.

As he raised the knife toward the sky, he knew just how far he was willing to go with God. And in that critical instant, the angel of the Lord cried out for him to halt, "for now I know that you fear God, since you have not withheld your son, your only son, from Me" (Gen. 22:12).

Through this practical test, he proved that loving God with all his heart was not just pious talk. As much as he loved Isaac, he loved God even more. No longer could he harbor doubts about the depth of his devotion. God already knew, but this test let Abraham know how much his faith had grown. Isaac on the altar proved that God's will for his life came before anything else.

Abraham also learned "God will provide" were more than empty words to a son's penetrating question. When the chips were down, God *did* provide. No one knows just how strongly Abraham believed that God would provide a substitute sacrifice. We do know that he was prepared to go ahead even though it meant the death of Isaac for "he considered that God is able to raise men even from the dead" (Heb. 11:19). At the right moment, God's ram was caught in the thicket and became the substitute for Isaac on the altar.

As a reminder that God would provide for His obedient children, Abraham renamed the location *Jehovah-jireh*, which means "the Lord will provide." Because God provided a substitute for Isaac, Abraham was able to descend the mount with him at his side, knowing that God had prevented a lonely journey home.

His trip up the mountain was not filled with joy—it was a hard road to travel. But once the peak had been reached and the command carried out, God reiterated and expanded His promise to make Abraham exceedingly fruitful and a blessing to the whole earth "because you have obeyed My voice" (Gen. 22:18).

He was not rewarded for blind unthinking obedience to an unreasonable demand. The leaf blown by the wind offers no resistance to the force of nature. But Abraham, the child of God, struggled with the decision and won over his own human resistance. That kind of obedience is blessed by God.

Abraham also learned to be thankful to God for what he had. We cannot even begin to imagine what went through his mind as he and Isaac returned from the mountain. The heavy heart that ascended toward the altar was now bursting with joy and thanksgiving to God.

Through this encounter, he learned something important—that life is a *gift*. Isaac was a free gift from God, one he had no claim on at all. God bound Himself to Abraham to give him a son and He did. Instead of appreciating him as a gift, Abraham thought of Isaac as belonging to Sarah and him.

God called him to Moriah to see if he was willing to return the gift which he had been given. But when he offered the gift back to God, he was permitted to keep it permanently. God gave Isaac to him a second time. If he loved Isaac before, imagine how much more he loved and appreciated him now. He knew that his most precious treasure was a free gift from God.

It was a lonely man who raised a knife over his son, ready to go all the way with God. But God halted the downward plunge and the dark clouds of loneliness lifted from his soul. Abraham went home rejoicing. His personal commitment to God brought joy and happiness to his soul.

One Step at a Time

Few of us know just how much Christ means to us. As we face new areas of commitment, we gain fresh insights as to how much we are willing to give to God. Most have made that big commitment called dedication—turning the total life over to Christ. But we still face the specific problems that must be committed to His control.

Daily we are confronted with new areas God wants us to make available to Him. He will not demand that we place everything on the line at once, but He prepares us for committing more of our lives to His control. Just as Abraham faced one area of trust at a time in preparation for Mount Moriah, we too are being prepared for our ultimate test of faith. Every little hurdle we overcome is preparation for the next one, till finally we are ready for the ultimate test. God does not ask us to go all the way with Him till we are ready.

We all struggle with personal commitment. We would be dishonest if we declared that we could sacrifice a personal desire to God without a struggle. The desire of the flesh to keep control of our lives never stops; the struggle will always precede any personal commitment.

But God does not move us along faster than we can respond. He won't ask us to jump a six-foot fence when we are still tripping over a two-footer. Or He won't ask us to give up a career for Him till we have learned to trust Him for our daily bread. God moves us at a pace unique for us and never asks more than we are able to give.

God will never ask us to give to Him more than He has given to us. "He who did not spare His own Son, but delivered Him up for us all, how will He not also with Him freely give us all things?" (Rom. 8:32) Because He loves us, He gave the Lord Jesus to die for us, and made it impossible for us to claim that God asks more than He gives.

Remember that everything is a gift from God— children, career, health, and wealth. Our problems come when we see ourselves as *owners* rather than *stewards*. When we realize that what God is asking us to give back is His anyway, we can be thankful that He ever let us have it in the first place.

What means more to you than anything else in the world? If God asked you to give that to Him now, could you? Would you give it to Him without hesitation or would you go through a lonely struggle before letting go? If He is asking you to sacrifice something to Him, say Yes—and experience the peace that will soothe your troubled soul.

I have some dear friends who had an experience similar to Abraham's. While their youngest son was in college, he felt called by God to emigrate to Israel and live among the Hebrew people in order to share Christ with them.

When his mother first received this news, she was considerably upset. But, as that day was still a couple of years away and there was a chance he